# Manufacturing Mobility

*A strategic guide to transferring manufacturing capability*

**Manufacturing Mobility**

First published in Great Britain 1999 by the University of Cambridge Institute for Manufacturing, Mill Lane, Cambridge CB2 1RX

**ISBN 1-902546-02-4**

# Contents

# Introduction

## *Who is this workbook for?*

This book has been written for managers in manufacturing companies who are involved in the transfer of production technology across geographical boundaries. Such transfers can range from dispatching drawings to an overseas subcontractor to moving the manufacturing capacity of an entire factory.

## *Why is it needed?*

International transfers of production technology can be extremely complicated and difficult to manage. In order for production capacity to be transferred swiftly and reliably between sites many different factors need to be considered. Unless a structure for managing these is developed, costly mistakes may be made.

## *What does it aim to do?*

This workbook provides a structure to assist in planning the international transfer of production technology. It does this by using a framework which links strategic considerations (e.g. Which country are you transferring to? What process are you going to transfer?) with implementation activities (e.g. What equipment needs to be transferred? How much training of the local workforce is required?) allowing potential problems to be identified early in the planning stages as well as various different scenarios to be considered.

## *How does it work?*

The book is divided into 4 sections:

- Section 1 - *An overview of the total process* - provides the basic concepts and structure of the workbook.
- Section 2 - *Where it all begins* - deals with the strategic considerations driving the need to transfer.
- Section 3 - *Doing it* - focuses on implementation activities.
- Section 4 - *Workpack* - consists of a series of worksheets designed to capture information relating to your project.

Each section is structured around a series of questions designed to be considered in the context of a specific transfer project.

Case study examples are provided throughout the workbook.

# AN OVERVIEW OF THE TOTAL PROCESS

# Background

The international transfer of production technology can involve anything from dispatching a set of engineering drawings to an overseas subcontractor to moving the manufacturing capability of a complete factory. In order to provide tools and techniques to support the range of possible transfers we need to have a common language to describe what is happening.

Figure 1 shows the variety of situations in which manufacturing transfers can take place.
The horizontal axis shows the relationship between the site sending the production technology and the site that is receiving it. This relationship may be one of customer to subcontractor, licensor to licensee, alliance partnership or plants within the same company.

The vertical axis represents the level of development that may be needed at the site receiving the technology. This development could be very minor (the transfer of a production process between similar plants) or very extensive (the construction of a complete new plant).

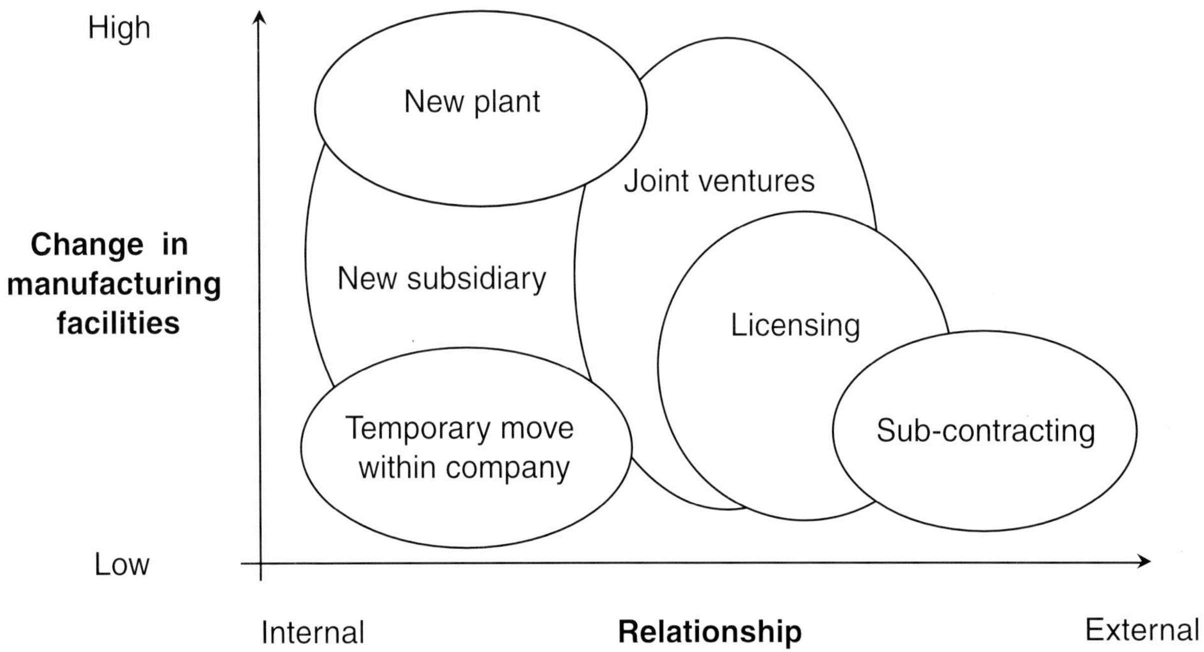


*Figure 1. The variety of situations in which a manufacturing transfer can take place*

From the range of possible types of transfer certain common elements can be identified (see Figure 2). These are:

- ✣ a home site which sends the production technology and
- ✣ a host site which receives it.

In addition, there will be:

- ✣ a channel or some form of link between the home and host sites. The nature of this channel strongly influences implementation activities associated with the transfer
- ✣ an agreed time-scale, or rate, for the transfer to be completed
- ✣ items of equipment and supplies that need to be transferred (although in some cases there is no 'hardware' to be transferred, just the 'software', i.e. knowledge)
- ✣ knowledge relating to the production process which the host site will need from the home site. Some of this knowledge may be well-documented (accurate engineering drawings) or relatively easy to document (detailed process descriptions). However, some of it may be much harder to transfer, e.g. the transfer of machining 'knack' or troubleshooting 'feel' that operators at the home site may have acquired over a long period of time.

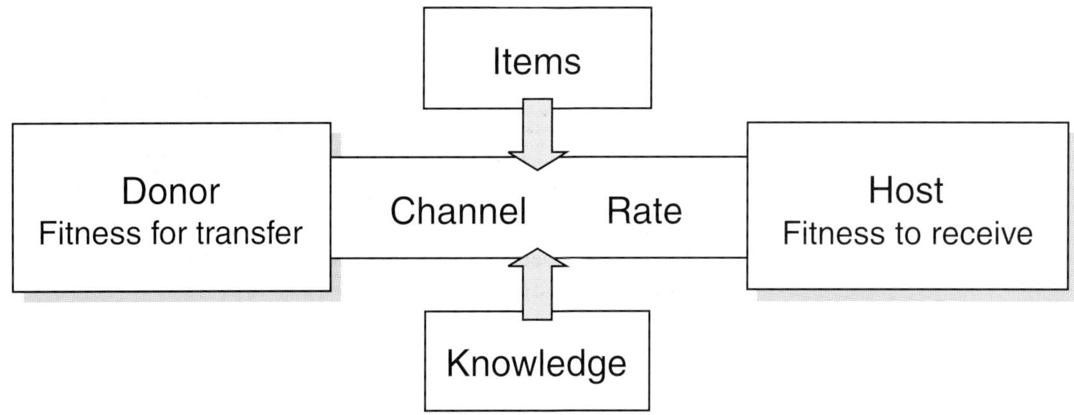


*Figure 2. Common elements that exist in all technology transfers*

## Stages of the transfer

The diagram (opposite) shows seven stages common to all transfers of production technology. Though these appear as discrete, in practice there is often a degree of overlap between the activities within each stage.

### *1. Strategy making*

The starting point for a transfer is consideration of the strategy that is driving the need to transfer a manufacturing process. At this stage attention is focused on thinking about *why* you want to transfer, and *what* you want to transfer. The motive for the transfer could be cost saving, proximity to customers or new market entry. The content of the transfer could be product components, a complete product or a range of products.

The remaining stages focus on implementing the transfer.

### *2. Exploring*

This will be strongly influenced by the 'why' and 'what' questions. In particular, if the transfer is from a site which is being closed down there will be specific problems in capturing knowledge and gaining co-operation from the home site.

At this stage attention is focused on identifying who the host for the manufacturing process might be. The choices are:

- a green-field development
- an existing subsidiary plant
- plant belonging to a completely new company (for example through a sub-contracting agreement a partnership or an acquisition)

Assessment of the suitability of potential host sites is carried out by 'profiling' their manufacturing capabilities. These are then compared with the home site's capabilities. From this it is usually possible to generate a short-list of possible host sites.

### *3. Assessing fitness for transfer*

Once a host, or set of possible hosts has been identified, the suitability of the manufacturing process and its ability to be transferred must be evaluated. During this stage the home site needs to evaluate the 'fitness for transfer' of the manufacturing process to be transferred. Fitness for transfer involves considering:

- how appropriate is a process for the host site
- how transferable is the manufacturing process

### *4. Packaging and adapting*

Once the fitness for transfer has been evaluated some modifications may be necessary. These activities can be grouped into:

- packaging, which refers to the change of format of some aspect of a manufacturing process (e.g. document translation).
- adapting, which involves some change to the process itself (e.g. using a different technology).

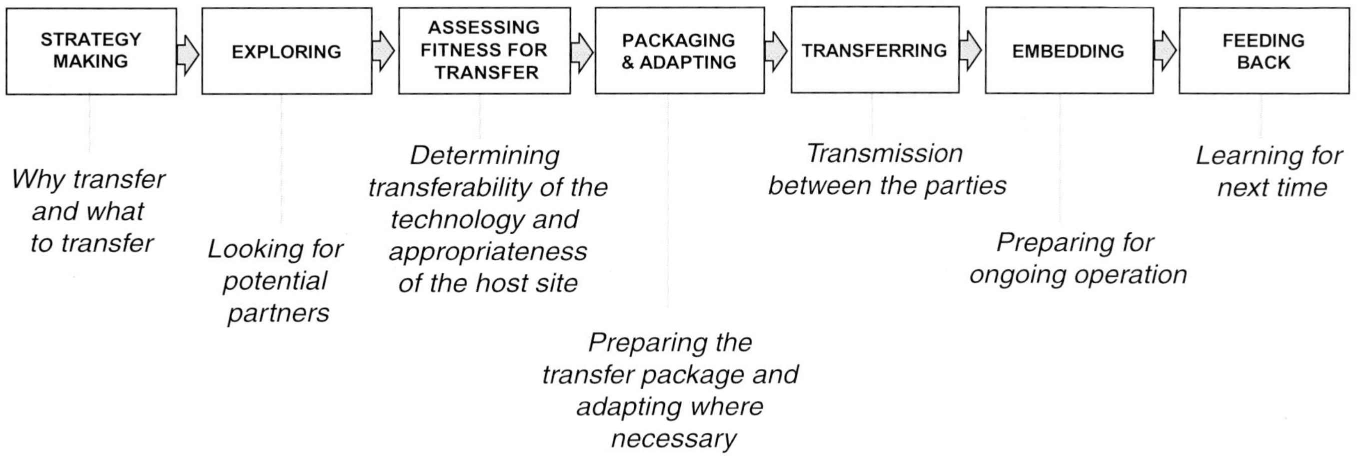


*Figure 3. Stages of the transfer process*

## 5. Transferring

Once the content of the transfer has been finalised the manufacturing process is ready to be moved. This stage usually involves more than just the shipment of equipment and documentation. It also includes the transfer of 'tacit' knowledge by training and the gradual phasing-in of packaged manufacturing technology (e.g. use of pilot plant and 'knock-down' production). These activities are usually based largely at the home site.

## 6. Embedding

This stage shifts the emphasis to activities at the host site. Embedding activities are those which allow the host to learn and assimilate in preparation for ongoing operations. For example, the host site needs to ensure that when support from the home site is reduced or withdrawn, it has sufficient knowledge to be able to continue operations. The level of activity at this stage depends on the type of transfer.

## 7. Feeding back

Once a degree of familiarity with the operation has been achieved by the host, the home site will typically ease back its level of involvement. There is often an appraisal stage after closure that both assesses the success of the project and captures learning from the transfer in a form that allows it to be used again the next time. Typically this stage will be given very limited attention. However, if the company wants to develop the ability to transfer production swiftly and reliably, it must learn from each of the transfers it carries out. The problem then becomes how best to capture the relevant knowledge to ensure that it is available next time.

## Manufacturing decision areas

We have shown how the transfer can be broken down into a number of stages. In order to see what activities are needed at each stage we need to divide these activities into a series of decision areas (Figure 4). These provide a way of grouping transfer activities in order to ensure that nothing is overlooked.

| Manufacturing Decision Area | Core Considerations |
|---|---|
| Facilities, capacity and technology | Manufacturing process description, building/site services, understanding manufacturing capabilities, capital equipment, modifications, technical support |
| Vertical integration and material supply | Lead-times, order book management, invoicing arrangements, material kitting and shipment policy, development of localisation plan |
| Production planning and material control | Data accuracy, definition of appropriate Bill of Materials structures, provision of support systems |
| Human resources | Skill requirements, selection and hiring, training plans, technical support |
| Knowledge | Document management, tacit knowledge, engineering change control, intellectual property rights |
| Organisational structure and relationships | Business processes, roles and responsibilities, reporting, dispute resolution |
| Quality | In-transit damage, targets, local supplier approval, reworks and returns |
| External environment | Customs and other potential delays, local infrastructure, legislative requirements |

*Figure 4. Manufacturing decision areas*

# Manufacturing transfer framework

Mapping the decision areas onto the stages of the transfer provides us with a framework for manufacturing transfers (Figure 5). This framework provides the structure for mapping the majority of the implementation activities in the remainder of this workbook.

**Stages of the transfer**

**Manufacturing decision areas**

| | *Exploring* | *Assessing* | *Packaging & adapting* | *Transferring* | *Embedding* | *Feeding back* |
|---|---|---|---|---|---|---|
| Facilities | | | | | | |
| Suppliers | | | | | | |
| Material control | | | | | | |
| Human resources | | | | | | |
| Knowledge | | | | | | |
| Organisation & relationships | | | | | | |
| Quality | | | | | | |
| External environment | | | | | | |

*Figure 5. A framework for manufacturing transfers*

## Structure of the workbook

In Section 2 we focus on the strategic considerations that underpin the international transfer of production technology.

Section 3 concentrates on the activities that need to be carried out to achieve these strategic goals. These activities are then reviewed and compared with the strategic aims of the transfer. Potential problems identified by examining the implementation activities can result in a reassessment of the strategic aims of the transfer.

The final section, the Workpack, consists of a set of worksheets which you should photocopy and use to capture information relating to your project.

*At the back of this workbook there is a series of worksheets for capturing information relating to your project.*

The workbook can be used in two ways:

✣ scenario planning – by assessing the activities required to implement different possible strategies, this workbook can be used to assess the costs and benefits of different options

✣ project planning – if the strategic considerations driving the need to transfer are fixed, then this workbook can be used to assist in the identification and management of the implementation activities at each stage of the transfer.

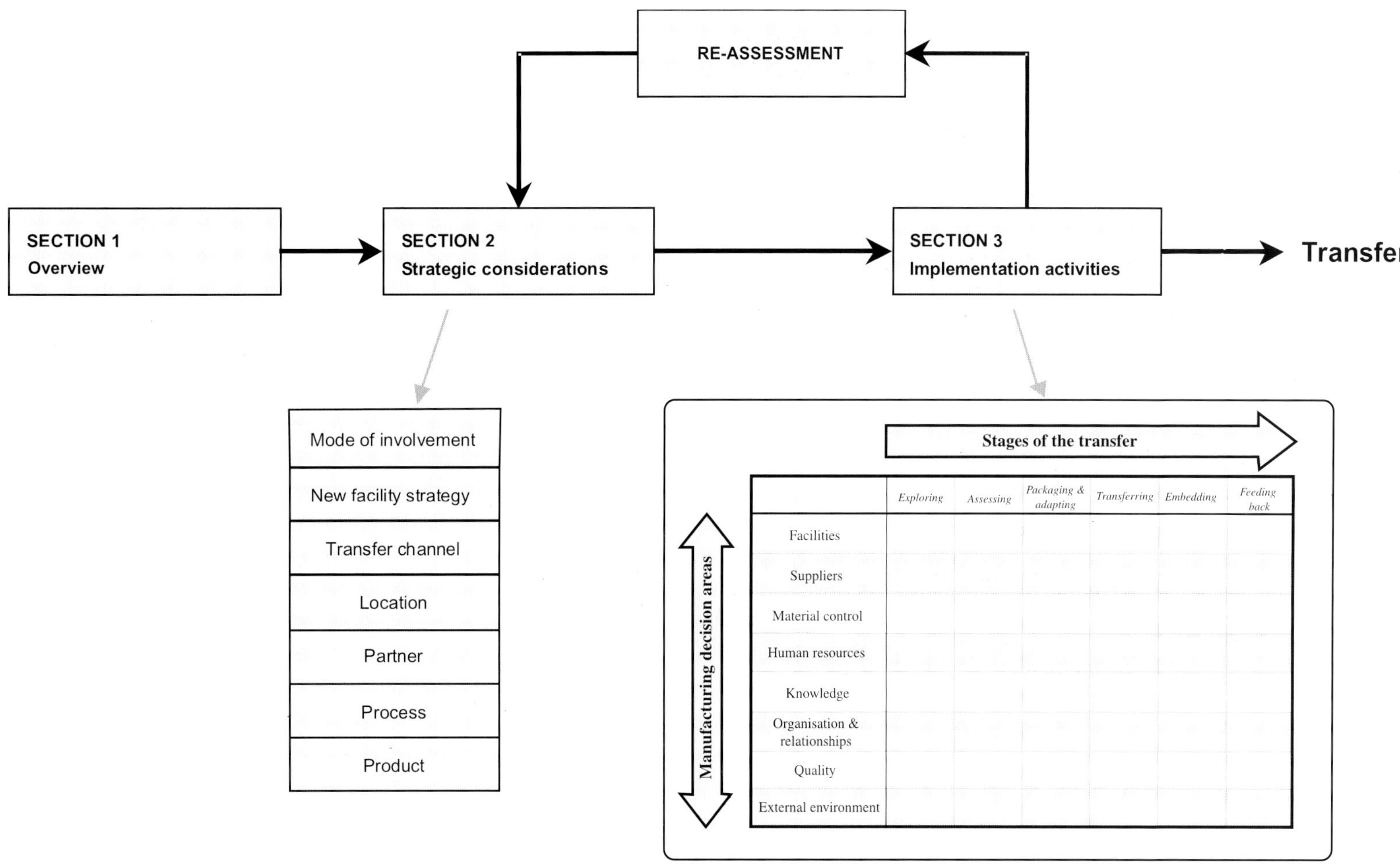


*Figure 6. Structure of the Manufacturing Mobility workbook*

# WHERE IT ALL BEGINS

## Strategic considerations

All transfers should begin by addressing the eight questions below. Use **Worksheet 1** to fill in the answers for your project and keep it to hand for easy reference.

### *Driving forces*

**What is driving the transfer of production overseas?**
There may be many factors pushing your firm to consider manufacturing overseas. These could include rising domestic costs, opportunities presented by new markets and the availability of certain skills. It is useful to make these explicit early in the process so that all involved understand the background to the project.

### *Mode of involvement*

**In what other way could these aims be achieved?**
Is the transfer of production the only way to achieve the strategic aims? It may be that the target overseas market could be served just as well by exporting rather than setting up local production. Has such an assessment been carried out and the various options identified?

### *New facilities strategy*

**What role is the host going to play in your strategy? Is this likely to change over time?**
If transfer is the preferred option it is important to consider the initial role of the host site and how this may change over time.

The three main motives for a transfer are:

1. Access to low cost factors of production
2. Use of local technological resources
3. Proximity to market

Based on these it is possible to identify six generic strategies for new overseas facilities depending on the extent of competence at the host site (see Figure 7).

### *Transfer channel*

**What is the relationship between the home and host site?**
Possibilities include:

- new subsidiary plant
- acquired plant
- joint venture
- license agreement
- purchaser of equipment

The choice of channel will influence the specific activities required to implement the transfer.

### *Location*

**Which country are you planning to transfer to?**
The culture and characteristics of the country in which the host site is located will probably have an impact on the outcome of the transfer. From the earliest possible stage it is important to consider potential problems that may occur as a result of differences in the characteristics of the home and host location.

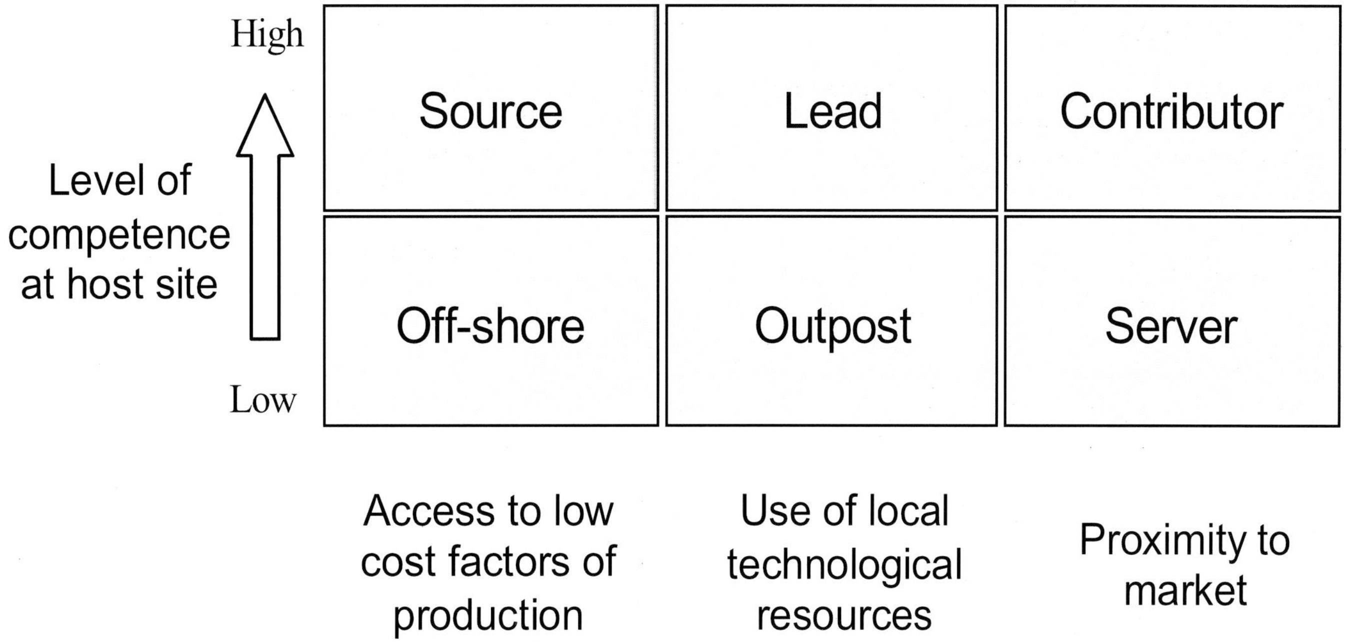


*Figure 7. The six generic strategies for new overseas facilities*

## *Partner*

**Do you have a partner or host in mind?**
It may be that this is not yet known. On the other hand a partner may have already been selected.

## *Product*

**Which product(s) will be transferred?**
Are you transferring a single product or a complete range?

## *Process*

**Which manufacturing process(es) will be transferred?**
Do you want to transfer the manufacture of a complete system, the assembly of sub-systems or the manufacture of components for assembly elsewhere?

Changing market conditions forced a Far Eastern multinational to close one of its manufacturing plants in mainland Europe and re-locate to the UK. This process required the codification of a complex manufacturing process at the redundant home site and its subsequent transfer to an existing host plant in the UK. The UK host and the home site had markedly different capabilities. As a result the transfer required the movement not only of capital equipment but also the re-establishment of a supplier network in the UK as well as the transfer of a substantial body of 'tacit' knowledge.

A European multinational sought to expand its operations in the US through the cloning of its UK manufacturing capability in the US. This required not only the assessment of how best to transfer the capability to the US, but also the determination of the effect that such a plant would have upon the global capabilities of the company.

# DOING IT - IMPLEMENTATION ACTIVITIES

# Exploring

*Aim: to produce a short-list of potential host sites*

### *Key questions*

How do I find potential host sites?
How do I assess potential host sites?

## *Finding potential host sites*

The key issue here is to ensure that the initial list of potential 'partners' in the selected geographical location matches the manufacturing capabilities required.

*Inputs*

- general understanding of the basic capabilities required by the product/process to be transferred
- country or region in which potential partners are sought
- host country specific sources such as trade organisations, embassies, trade delegations
- industry specific sources such as trade shows, industry catalogues and directories, industry associations
- other sources (e.g. internet searches)

You should use as many relevant data sources as possible and draw up a list of companies who possess the basic capabilities needed for the product/process which is being transferred. The tasks are:

- identify existing data sources and contacts used in the past (**Worksheet 2**)
- expand the list, if necessary, to provide the required coverage
- search the information for potential candidates
- log contact details for subsequent use

*Outputs*

- list of 5-10 companies meeting the basic criteria together with useful data sources for future reference.

Subsequent actions

Contact potential candidates to gather basic information about their business and to eliminate unsuitable ones. If insufficient candidates are identified, consider widening the search area (e.g. to other countries) or review the practicality (i.e. scope) of the transfer that you are planning.

## *Assessing potential host sites*

Once a short-list of potential sites has been drawn up compare the manufacturing capabilities at these sites with those at the home site. This should be carried out at different levels of detail to 'filter out' the unsuitable sites.

*Gathering basic partner data*

Basic, non-technical information relating to the potential partner sites can be gathered remotely. Using **Worksheet 3** as a faxback form, contact potential host sites and draw up a list of those which best fit your broad requirements.

*Building up a profile of manufacturing capabilities*

Prepare a more detailed profile of the manufacturing capabilities of the companies on your short list. Record your findings on **Worksheet 4.** An example of a partly completed worksheet is shown in Fig 8 opposite.

# Capability profile

## 1. Facilities, capacity and technology

| | | | | | | | | | Notes | |
|---|---|---|---|---|---|---|---|---|---|---|
| | | | | | | | | | Home | Partner |
| 1.1 | Shop layout | Flowline | | | | | | Job shop | | |
| 1.2 | Level of product/process technology | High | | | | | | Low | | |
| 1.3 | Level of capital investment | High | | | | | | Low | | |
| 1.4 | Availability of tooling | High | | | | | | Low | | |
| 1.5 | Availability of test equipment | High | | | | | | Low | | |
| 1.6 | Availability of secondary process equipment | High | | | | | | Low | | |
| 1.7 | General shopfloor cleanliness | High | | | | | | Low | | |
| 1.8 | Requirements for special environmental conditions (temperature, anti-static, dust, light) | High | | | | | | Low | | |
| 1.9 | Handling requirements (e.g. lifting capacity) | Heavy duty | | | | | | Manual | | |
| 1.10 | Material flow | Complex | | | | | | Simple | | |
| 1.11 | Maintenance capability | High | | | | | | Low | | |
| 1.12 | Capacity (units per day) | High | | | | | | Low | | |
| 1.13 | Capacity flexibility (+/- in one month) | High | | | | | | Low | | |

*Figure 8. Example of a part-completed Worksheet 4*

home site — proposed host site

Visit potential host sites to gather data on their capabilities. The results should be profiled against the home site. As you collect information on potential host sites make sure you cover the following manufacturing decision areas and record your findings on the relevant section of **Worksheet 4**:

- **Facilities, capacity and technology**
  Layout, level of process technology, level of investment, availability of tooling and test equipment, cleanliness, requirements for special environmental conditions, handling requirements.
- **Suppliers**
  Proximity, reliability and capabilities of local suppliers, material lead-times and general span of process.
- **Material control**
  Process choice, control philosophy, number of products, batch sizes, scheduling systems, material storage and control.
- **Human resources**
  Workforce size, skill level, employment and working conditions, level of temporary staff, level of availability, job definition, supervisory structure, motivation and union representation.
- **Knowledge**
  Awareness of tacit knowledge issues, ability to deal with documentation, documentation control, change control, use of IT systems.
- **Organisation and relationships**
  Size of organisation, type of organisation, relationships with other companies (owner, subsidiary, etc.), alliance partners.
- **Quality**
  Quality systems, process control capability and inspection capability.
- **External environment**
  Political and economic situation, exchange rates, utilities, transportation and communications.

Finding partner sites with exact matching capabilities can be extremely difficult. Often the capabilities of a potential host may have to be supported by the use of sub-contractors. For example, the home site in a UK to US transfer of machinery had in-house electrolysis nickel plating capability, whereas the host did not. The home site needed to spend time during the exploring phase helping the would-be host find sub-contractors with plating capabilities that would deliver appropriate finish and tolerance.

Differing manufacturing 'philosophies' can have a strong impact upon how partner sites are likely to be able to work together. For example, a UK manufacturer of electronic equipment offered high levels of configurability at fairly low production volumes but with manufacture to customer order. The planned host site focussed on high volume production with little configurability. These underlying differences in the way production was undertaken turned out to be the cause of a number of problems later in the transfer.

*At the end of this stage you will have a short-list of preferred host sites to choose from with details of the manufacturing capabilities of each.*

# Assessing fitness for transfer

*Aim: to assess the suitability of the manufacturing process for use as the host site*

### *Key question*

How do I measure the transferability and appropriateness of a manufacturing process?

The profile of manufacturing capabilities developed previously provides a rough comparison of capabilities at the home and host site. The aim of this section is to assess the host site in terms of the specific capabilities required by the manufacturing process which is to be transferred.

## *Transferability*

The first characteristic to be evaluated and assessed is the ease with which the manufacturing process can be transferred from its current home site.

**Transferability** is assessed using the categories below. These should be captured using **Worksheet 5**. The activities identified here will overlap to a large extent with those in the next stage – 'Packaging and adapting'.

### *Knowledge*

- amount and stage of knowledge
- dependence on truly tacit knowledge
- teachability of knowledge
- knowledge gained from previous transfers

### *Customised and obsolete processes*

- whether the technology is customised, redundant or obsolete
- extent to which the documentation is up-to-date and representative

### *Process adaptability*

- availability of alternatives
- need for a pilot

### *Packaging for transfer*

- use of semi-knock down (SKD) or complete knock down (CKD)
- potential for splitting into sub-processes
- protecting intellectual property rights (IPR)

## *Appropriateness*

The categories used for assessing **appropriateness** are described below. Each of these areas should be looked at in terms of the product/process to be transferred to provide an indication of the level of appropriateness for the intended location. Use copies of **Worksheet 6** to profile both the process to be transferred and the host site.

### *Host labour*

- productivity and cost of direct and indirect labour
- skills available from local labour pool
- education and language characteristics
- labour turnover

### *Target market*

- extent to which process capacity and flexibility match target market and demand characteristics

*A separate workbook entitled **Fitness for Transfer** is published by the Institute for Manufacturing and provides a detailed assessment of the 'fitness for transfer' of a manufacturing process. Here we give a simplified version of this assessment. However, it is strongly recommended that a more detailed assessment, using the workbook **Fitness for Transfer**, is carried out prior to any transfer.*

- match between product and the needs of the target market

*Suppliers*

- quality, cost, delivery, flexibility and service of local or international suppliers

*Host infrastructure*

- quality, cost and availability of local utilities
- availability, cost and reliability of telecommunications, road, rail, shipping and airfreight infrastructure
- space and format of buildings

*Host organisation's resources and capabilities*

- technical resources
- familiarity with manufacturing methods
- support capabilities
- organisational structure

*Host culture*

- individualism and uncertainty avoidance
- power distance
- work practices
- approach to problem solving and quality perception

*Host environment*

- local temperature range, humidity and air quality

*Financing*

- cost of inventory, land and capital and foreign exchange requirements

*Host government / legal requirements*

- Legal demands, import duties and quotas, labour law, approval and licence requirements, government emission regulations and planning laws.

Basic issues such as different drawing practices and units of measurement at home and host sites can lead to difficulties in the transfer. For example, unforeseen delays in a transfer from the UK to the US were found to have been caused by the lack of readily available metric fasteners in the US. The time required to re-machine and find ways to 'make-do' was much longer than anticipated. Annotating the drawings from the UK site to show where modifications could be made also led to delays.

The external environment may impact upon the production process at the host site in unexpected ways. For example, higher levels of humidity at the Asian host site than at the UK home site caused quality problems for one transfer of electronic display components. Coating processes in particular can be problematic when transferred between markedly different climates.

*At the end of this stage you will have an indication of how transferable a manufacturing process is as well as some measure of its appropriateness for the host site. Based on these assessments the emphasis moves to 'packaging and adapting'.*

# Packaging and adapting

*Aim: to determine how the manufacturing process needs to be altered to suit the host site*

### *Key question*

What adaptations to the process are needed?

## *Facilities*

The transferability and appropriateness assessments carried out in the previous section will have identified areas where changes are required in the manufacturing process to facilitate the transfer. These changes may affect the format of the process (e.g. documents that need to be translated) or even the process itself (e.g. the use of a new technology).

## *Suppliers*

The transfer plan needs to take into account the capabilities of host site suppliers and ways in which these may need to be enhanced to suit the process. Alternatively the process itself may have to be redesigned to cope with the requirements of local suppliers. In such cases the best solution may be to source suppliers initially from the host site. The design of the transfer needs to consider the implications of a gradual shift to local sourcing.

## *Material control*

In designing the transfer package the home site must be aware of the way in which parts and material are controlled at the host site. The assumption that the host site will adapt often leads to problems - the "not invented here" syndrome is commonly observed. The home site may need to accept that the production process is embedded in a site where there are different approaches to data accuracy and the provision of support systems.

## *Human resources*

Having already assessed the level of operator and supervisory skills required by the process, the design of the transfer package needs to include mechanisms for ensuring that these skills are available at the host site. Such mechanisms may include training programmes, selection and hiring criteria, transfer of personnel from the home site and the provision of on-going technical support.

## *Knowledge*

Although the tacit elements of a manufacturing process may present the biggest problem for a transfer, the explicit (documented) knowledge may also cause difficulties. For example if home and host site use different CAD systems (or even different projections for their engineering drawings) this may be a major problem for the transfer.

## *Organisations and relationships*

During the packaging phase the links between the home and host sites need to be clear and open. Successful preparation of the process for transfer requires open communication between the two sites. In particular there need to be unchanging 'gatekeepers' at both home and host sites to ensure a regular and reliable exchange of information.

## *Quality*

As the transfer package is designed it is important to consider the minimum standards for transportation of key items. Even if the transfer is purely a 'soft' one (i.e. it contains no physical items) provision still needs to be made for an assessment of acceptable quality at the host site.

## *External environment*

The transfer needs to take into account any major environmental differences between the home and host site. For example, high levels of humidity can affect coating processes.

# Options for packaging and adapting

In the light of all these factors, you should consider the following issues:

- Transferring the process in different stages by the use of 'knock-down' modes of transfer. This can be helpful if the host site lacks some of the required capabilities. Knock-down modes enable transfer to take place in stages whilst the host site capabilities are being developed.
- If earlier assessments have indicated that the manufacturing capability of the host site is inadequate for the process it may be impossible (or at least extremely costly) to make the transfer. In such situations seek out alternative technologies, methods and processes that are more appropriate to the host facility. Companies taking this option should pilot the new process to ensure that appropriate levels of output and quality can be maintained.

The type of transfer will have an impact upon this stage. If the transfer is the result of a plant closure then there will be specific issues to deal with. For example, the planned closure of a manufacturing plant in mainland Europe was to result in the transfer of manufacturing capability to the UK. The home site provided no support for this transfer. It was only through finding employment for key home site individuals at the host site that the project manager was able to access and transfer any of the tacit manufacturing knowledge

The differences between the workforces in North and Central America led to a number of issues during the packaging and adapting of one manufacturing process. The high level of labour turnover at the host site posed challenges for the training programmes required to support the transfer of a complex process. By updating and adapting the documentation (in particular by the increased use of graphics and colour keys) the home site was able to speed the training of the host site workforce.

*At the end of this stage you will have determined the necessary changes to the product and process to make them readily transferable. Next we examine issues relating to the transfer itself.*

# Transferring

*Aim: to identify what items and knowledge need to be transferred.*

## *Key question*

What do I need to transfer, how and when?

The content of the transfer can be divided broadly into physical **items** (equipment, materials) and **knowledge** (documentation, 'know-how'). These are discussed below under the headings of the various manufacturing decision areas. **Worksheet 7** provides a structure for capturing and categorising the items and knowledge to be transferred. It is recommended that some estimate of preparation and transfer time be included for each.

## *Facilities*

Earlier assessments have identified the equipment that is needed at the host site. Where investment in capital equipment is necessary, decisions need to be made on the relative merits of using redundant or spare assets as opposed to making new purchases which may well involve the preparation of detailed installation and commissioning plans.

## *Suppliers*

Many transfer problems at this stage centre around secondary lead-times, i.e. the coordination of activities of both home and host suppliers as the production process is transferred and ramped-up to full operation at the host site. If host site suppliers are unable to meet the requirements of the process to be transferred, then you will need to consider capacity limits when sourcing supplies from the home site.

## *Material control*

As the transfer may involve the transition from SKD to CKD and then local sourcing, the material and parts control element of the transfer must be designed to cope with this ramping-up of activity. In the early stages a very high percentage of the materials may need to be shipped from the home site.

## *Human resources*

The design of the transfer should take into account the human resource capabilities of the host site including any extra training and development needed. During the transfer phase, selection and hiring should be linked to training needs. One of the most effective (though costly) mechanisms for training is the exchange of personnel between the home and host sites.

## *Knowledge*

There are a number of ways to transfer knowledge between the home and host site. The choice depends on many factors including the type of knowledge, the resources available and the desired speed of the transfer. For example, the fastest way to transfer details of a complex component assembly may be by transferring personnel. This can result in very high costs. An alternative is to use video and photographs which for certain kinds of knowledge transfer may be an effective, lower cost option.

## *Organisations and relationships*

During the transfer phase problems may occur which require fast resolution. If no mechanisms are in place to address these issues, either the home or host site may resort to ad hoc solutions. These can cause further problems in the long term.

## *Quality*

The potential for in-transit damage, particularly when SKD and CKD modes are being used, needs to be identified as early as possible and fed back to the home site to allow the preparation of contingency plans. This highlights the need for effective return loops to be included in the business process definitions.

## *External environment*

During the transfer itself the most common problems under this heading seem to be those relating to customs. There needs to be an assessment of worst-case and routine expectations for customs clearance with provision and agreement on responsibility for expediting delays.

The nature of the underlying relationship between home and host sites can lead to complications in transfers. A transfer of the production of electronic equipment from the UK to China involved three separate organisations: the joint venture in China, the home site in the UK and the local representative company of the home site company in China. This complicated many business processes (in particular, invoicing) and required careful thought to develop practical mechanisms for dispute resolution.

In many transfers delays caused by slow customs clearance can be very disruptive. For one transfer to the Far East the use of a local agent was found to be invaluable in overcoming such delays.

---

*At the end of this stage you will know which items and what knowledge are needed at the host site and have some indication of the costs and timings involved. From this analysis you should be able to highlight those areas where considerable resource is needed to carry out the transfer successfully.*

---

# Embedding

*Aim: to ensure full understanding of the manufacturing process at the host site so that operations can continue successfully when home site support is withdrawn.*

## *Key question*

What level of support is needed from the home site and for how long?

While the exact level and quality of support required at the host site depends on the type of transfer, some general observations can be made. **Worksheet 8** provides a structure for capturing likely problem areas that may require dedicated resources for an extended period of time.

## *Facilities*

During the embedding phase the focus of activity shifts from the home to the host site. If the host site has little or no experience in using the transferred equipment a high level of support will be needed from the home site. This may include training for both operating and technical support personnel. If the equipment is complex and/or has been customised, then the level of support from the home site will probably remain high for a substantial period of time.

## *Suppliers*

As the activities at the host site are ramped-up, the new facility must ensure that local suppliers develop appropriate capability so that they can deliver to the same standards as those at the home site. This may require direct links between home and host site suppliers.

## *Material control*

New approaches to material and parts flow may need to be developed. The home site should remain closely involved with these to ensure that quality and data accuracy is maintained.

## *Human resources*

As the host site moves to full operation, the level of support from the home site will decrease. Training programmes should have ensured that local skills have reached an appropriate level to cope with this. In addition the host site must ensure that it can retain the core skills needed for continued operation regardless of likely levels of labour turnover.

## *Knowledge*

The design of the transfer package should indicate the mechanisms for the transfer of knowledge. You should also ensure that the knowledge is effectively embedded at the host site. Technical support from the home site may only be available for a limited period of time. Modifications made at the host site need to be fed back to the home site to ensure that documentation is consistent and up-to-date.

## *Organisations and relationships*

Much emphasis may have been placed on ensuring open communications between home and host site during the

transfer and this needs to be maintained during the embedding phase. The relationship between the two sites may change over time and this can have an impact upon the level and mechanism of communication between them.

## *Quality*

The design of the transfer package should have included provision for the assessment of acceptable standards as the host site ramps up to full-scale production. Included in this should be an assessment of host site suppliers together with any corrective action needed if a problem is identified.

## *External environment*

Even though the process of embedding at the host site has progressed well, many transfers (particularly those to developing countries) have come to grief over worse than expected conditions of roads (impacting upon supplies and shipments), utilities (in particular, reliability of power supplies) and communications. Contingency plans need to be developed to cope with such eventualities.

The agreement as to when a transfer is complete can lead to disputes. The sign-off of a transfer from Europe to the Far East took much longer than anticipated because of late-stage arguments over the original contract.

Once a process has been transferred it may be further adapted in the light of local conditions at the host site. In addition, the process may continue to be modified at the home site. One transfer from Europe to China found the final stages of the transfer complicated by the inadequacy of the processes for tracking and controlling engineering drawings in the light of frequent changes at both the home and host sites.

---

*At the end of this stage the level of support required at the host site and likely problem areas will have been identified.*

---

# Feeding back

*Aim: to ensure that the experience of the transfer is captured and stored in a format that will allow ready access for future transfers.*

## *Key questions*

What needs to be captured?
What is the best way to store this?

The experience of the transfer needs to be captured at both the home and host sites. This will allow the organisation to build up competence for the future transfer of production technology.

## *Facilities*

The process by which equipment has been adapted for use at a particular location may be extremely useful for the firm in undertaking future transfers. Capture what has happened at the home site and also monitor how things have changed at the host site over time.

## *Suppliers*

Co-ordinating secondary lead-times can be particularly problematic for transfers. Many difficulties only become apparent during the implementation stages. Experience gained in managing such problems and developing localisation plans for suppliers will be invaluable to both the home and host sites - but only if it has been captured and stored in a format where it can be readily accessed in the future.

## *Material control*

The home site may be able to learn from the internal operations at the host site. It may be that the host site needs to adapt its processes over time to bring them more into line with the home site. There is, therefore, a need to capture the experience of how this adaptation has been managed.

## *Human resources*

Knowledge of local practice and custom at the host site may be a valuable resource for the home site. In addition, the experience of adapting and developing a production process for different levels of operator input can prove invaluable in helping the home site to understand its own capabilities.

## *Knowledge*

Capturing experience from the transfer needs to address three questions: Were the knowledge mechanisms used appropriate and effective? Was the right knowledge transferred? How has the knowledge been adapted at the host site?

## *Organisations and relationships*

The ability to exchange knowledge with external organisations can be regarded as a key capability for a firm engaged in international manufacturing. This capability can be developed over time, but requires in-built processes to ensure that learning takes place whenever a transfer is effected. Experience developed when working in partnerships can be invaluable.

## *Quality*

Assessment of 'quality critical' areas forms the key component of a transfer design package. The home site needs to have the ability to assess such areas and design appropriate business processes to ensure that quality is maintained during the transfer and at the host site. This ability needs to be recognised and supported at the home site so that transfers to a range of possible host sites can be effectively carried out in the future.

## *External environment*

Knowledge of local conditions gleaned from the host site provides a valuable resource for future transfers. However, such information can become quickly out-of-date. The home site needs to ensure that it has access to up-to-date information on particular regions and that this is available when and where it is most needed.

# How to capture this knowledge?

Much of the experience of a transfer typically remains within the heads of those involved in the project. It is unusual for time and resource to be allocated to capture experience of a transfer so that it can be accessed in the future. When attempts are made, the manner in which the knowledge is captured (typically by writing detailed notes which are then filed away) often means that it is never put to good use. In addition, the material is frequently in a format applicable to one specific transfer and it may be hard to see how general lessons can be drawn for the future.
The structure used in this workbook means that the completed worksheets used for one transfer could be used for comparison with a markedly different transfer. In addition, this structure lends itself to the linked document approach used by Internet browsers. A prototype software application has been developed by the Centre for International Manufacturing that allows experience from transfers to be captured 'on-the-fly'. For further information contact the Institute for Manufacturing at the address on the back cover of this workbook.

A number of the transfers observed during the development of this workbook used the researchers' case studies as a means of capturing experience about their own transfers. These short reports, written on the basis of interviews carried out within the company, provided a structured, neutral view of the issues faced during the transfer and how these were addressed.

---

*On completion of this stage you will have identified aspects of the transfer that you wish to record for future reference and ways of achieving this.*

---

# Re-assessment

In Section 2 we captured the strategic drivers that underpin the desire to transfer production technology.

In this section we have captured and structured the various implementation activities that are required for those strategic aims to be realised.

We need now to compare the implementation activities with the strategic goals in order to assess whether the costs of these activities outweigh the potential gains from the strategy.

Any issues arising from the review of the implementation of the transfer should be looked at within the context of the strategic aims of the project.

If insurmountable problems are revealed that are likely to prevent the efficient transfer of production, it may be necessary to modify the strategic aims of the project.

A European producer of heavy electrical equipment sought to build on growing demand in the US by transferring production to North America. Examination of the manufacturing process at the home site using the stages outlined in this workbook revealed the very low level of transferability of the process. The costs were shown to be so high that they countered the potential benefits of having production located within this market. The firm decided instead to build up local marketing and support resources for the product.

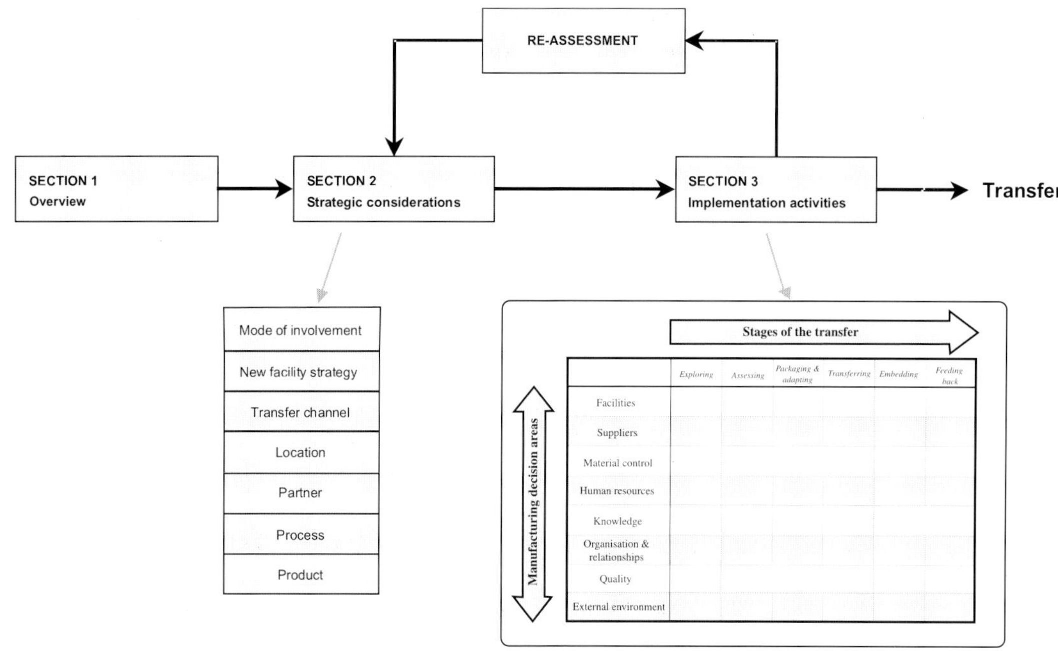

# MANUFACTURING MOBILITY WORKPACK

## Worksheet 1. Strategic considerations

### Driving forces

- What is driving the transfer of production overseas?

### Mode of involvement

- In what other ways could these aims be achieved?

### New facilities strategy

- What role is the host going to play in the strategy of the home site?
- Is this likely to change over time?

### Transfer channel

- What is the relationship between the home and host site?

### Location

- Which country are you planning to transfer to?

### Partner

- Do you have a partner or host in mind?

### Product

- Which product(s) will be transferred?

### Process

- Which manufacturing process(es) will be transferred?

## Worksheet 2. Creating a partner shortlist *a) potential sources of information*

| Source | Contact details (address, telephone, fax, e-mail) | Geographical coverage | Industry coverage | Cost | Usefulness (high/medium/low) |
|---|---|---|---|---|---|
| | | | | | |
| | | | | | |
| | | | | | |
| | | | | | |
| | | | | | |
| | | | | | |
| | | | | | |
| | | | | | |
| | | | | | |
| | | | | | |
| | | | | | |
| | | | | | |
| | | | | | |
| | | | | | |
| | | | | | |
| | | | | | |
| | | | | | |
| | | | | | |

## **Worksheet 2. Creating a partner shortlist** *b) results of search*

| Company name | Address | Telephone<br>Fax<br>e-mail | Contact name | Apparent match with desired capabilities (high/medium/low) | Source of information |
|---|---|---|---|---|---|
| | | | | | |
| | | | | | |
| | | | | | |
| | | | | | |
| | | | | | |
| | | | | | |
| | | | | | |
| | | | | | |
| | | | | | |
| | | | | | |
| | | | | | |
| | | | | | |
| | | | | | |
| | | | | | |
| | | | | | |
| | | | | | |
| | | | | | |

## Worksheet 3. Basic partner data

# 1. General business information

Company name

Address

Telephone Fax

Contact for future correspondence

Position

Ownership details

Age of company

Associated companies (e.g. sister, parent, subsidiary)

Annual sales (turnover)

Product portfolio

Major customers

## Worksheet 3. Basic partner data *continued*

# 2. Facilities

| | |
|---|---|
| Number of manufacturing sites | |
| | |
| Total office area | |
| Total manufacturing area | |

# 3. Basic manufacturing capabilities

| | | Notes |
|---|---|---|
| Casting | YES / NO | |
| Forging | YES / NO | |
| Extrusion | YES / NO | |
| Turning | YES / NO | |
| Boring | YES / NO | |
| Milling | YES / NO | |
| Grinding | YES / NO | |
| Sheet / plate fabrication | YES / NO | |
| Electro / electroless plating | YES / NO | |
| Heat treatment | YES / NO | |
| Assembly | YES / NO | |
| Lifting capacity (specify) | | |
| Painting | YES / NO | |
| Packaging | YES / NO | |

**Worksheet 3. Basic partner data** *continued*

# 4. Suppliers

| | In-country | Overseas |
|---|---|---|
| Number of suppliers: | | |
| raw materials (e.g. steel) | | |
| proprietary items (e.g. motors) | | |
| commodities (e.g. fasteners) | | |
| Average delivery leadtimes: | | |
| raw materials (e.g. steel) | | |
| proprietary items (e.g. motors) | | |
| commodities (e.g. fasteners) | | |

# 5. Human Resources

| | Number of employees | | | |
|---|---|---|---|---|
| | Full time | Part time | Temporary | Basic working hours / week |
| Indirect staff | | | | |
| Direct operators | | | | |

# 6. Quality

| | |
|---|---|
| Quality accreditation / awards held | |
| Inspection facilities available | |

# 7. Any other information

**Worksheet 4. Manufacturing capability profile**

# Capability profile

## 1. Facilities, capacity and technology

| | | | | | | | | | Notes home | Notes partner |
|---|---|---|---|---|---|---|---|---|---|---|
| 1.1 | Shop layout | flowline | | | | | | job shop | | |
| 1.2 | Level of product/process technology | high | | | | | | low | | |
| 1.3 | Level of capital investment | high | | | | | | low | | |
| 1.4 | Availability of tooling | high | | | | | | low | | |
| 1.5 | Availability of test equipment | high | | | | | | low | | |
| 1.6 | Availability of secondary process equipment | high | | | | | | low | | |
| 1.7 | General shopfloor cleanliness | high | | | | | | low | | |
| 1.8 | Requirements for special environmental conditions (temperature, anti-static, dust, light) | high | | | | | | low | | |
| 1.9 | Handling requirements (e.g. lifting capacity) | heavy duty | | | | | | manual | | |
| 1.10 | Material flow | complex | | | | | | simple | | |
| 1.11 | Maintenance capability | high | | | | | | low | | |
| 1.12 | Capacity (units per day) | high | | | | | | low | | |
| 1.13 | Capacity flexibility (+/- in one month) | high | | | | | | low | | |

## Worksheet 4. Manufacturing capability profile *continued*

# 2. Suppliers

| | | | | | | | | Notes home | Notes partner |
|---|---|---|---|---|---|---|---|---|---|
| 2.1 Span of process | wide | | | | | | narrow | | |
| 2.2 Use of intermittent external process stages | none | | | | | | common | | |
| 2.3 Material availability (proximity of suppliers) | local | | | | | | global | | |
| 2.4 Material leadtimes | short | | | | | | long | | |
| 2.5 Delivery reliability | good | | | | | | poor | | |
| 2.6 Supplier relationships | single sources | | | | | | multiple sources | | |
| 2.7 Local supplier capabilities | high | | | | | | low | | |

# 3. Material control

| | | | | | | | | Notes home | Notes partner |
|---|---|---|---|---|---|---|---|---|---|
| 3.1 Process choice | flowline | | | | | | project/jobbing | | |
| 3.2 Control philosophy | pull | | | | | | push | | |
| 3.3 Number of different products | high | | | | | | low | | |
| 3.4 Minimum batch size | low | | | | | | high | | |
| 3.5 Scheduling systems | automated | | | | | | manual | | |
| 3.6 Material storage | lineside | | | | | | separate stores | | |
| 3.7 Material control | tight | | | | | | loose | | |

## Worksheet 4. Manufacturing capability profile *continued*

# 4. Human resources

| | | | | | | | | | Notes home | Notes partner |
|---|---|---|---|---|---|---|---|---|---|---|
| 4.1 | Workforce size | large | | | | | | small | | |
| 4.2 | Skill levels / education: | | | | | | | | | |
| | management | high | | | | | | low | | |
| | supervisors | high | | | | | | low | | |
| | operators | high | | | | | | low | | |
| 4.3 | Employment conditions | generous | | | | | | poor | | |
| 4.4 | Working conditions | good | | | | | | poor | | |
| 4.5 | Level of temporary staff | low | | | | | | high | | |
| 4.6 | Labour availability: | | | | | | | | | |
| | volume | high | | | | | | low | | |
| | skill | high | | | | | | low | | |
| 4.7 | Job definition | flexible | | | | | | dedicated | | |
| 4.8 | Supervisory structure | flat | | | | | | hierarchical | | |
| 4.9 | Motivation | high | | | | | | low | | |
| 4.10 | Union representation | negligible | | | | | | full | | |

## Worksheet 4. Manufacturing capability profile *continued*

# 5. Knowledge

| | | | | | | | | | Notes home | Notes partner |
|---|---|---|---|---|---|---|---|---|---|---|
| 5.1 | Ability to deal with tacit knowledge | high | | | | | | low | | |
| 5.2 | Ability to deal with documentation (format, language, detail etc.) | high | | | | | | low | | |
| 5.3 | Documentation control | tight | | | | | | loose | | |
| 5.4 | Change control | tight | | | | | | weak | | |
| 5.5 | Use of IT systems | wide spread | | | | | | negligible | | |

# 6. Organisation and relationships

6.1 Size of organisation (turnover, workforce size)

6.2 Type of organisation (e.g. in-house manufacturer, subcontractor)

6.3 Relationships with other companies (e.g. subsidiary, owner etc.)

6.4 Key alliance partners

## Worksheet 4. Manufacturing capability profile *continued*

# 7. Quality

| | | | | | | | | | Notes home | Notes partner |
|---|---|---|---|---|---|---|---|---|---|---|
| 7.1 | Quality systems | advanced | | | | | | poor | | |
| 7.2 | Process control capability | advanced | | | | | | poor | | |
| 7.3 | Inspection capability | advanced | | | | | | poor | | |

# 8. External environment

| | | | | | | | | | Notes home | Notes partner |
|---|---|---|---|---|---|---|---|---|---|---|
| 8.1 | Political situation | stable | | | | | | unstable | | |
| 8.2 | Economic situation | stable | | | | | | unstable | | |
| 8.3 | Exchange rates | stable | | | | | | unstable | | |
| 8.4 | Currency conversion | easy | | | | | | difficult | | |
| 8.5 | Utilities | reliable | | | | | | unreliable | | |
| 8.6 | Telecommunications | reliable | | | | | | unreliable | | |
| 8.7 | Transport links | good | | | | | | poor | | |
| 8.8 | Inflation rates (per annum) | low | | | | | | high | | |

# Worksheet 5. Measuring transferability

<table>
<tr><th></th><th colspan="3">Dimensions</th></tr>
<tr><th>Key factors<br>*Properties*</th><th>Totally non-transferable</th><th>---------</th><th>Totally transferable</th></tr>
<tr><td>**Knowledge issues**</td><td></td><td></td><td></td></tr>
<tr><td>*Amount and stage of knowledge*</td><td>ignorance</td><td>|------|------|------|------|</td><td>science</td></tr>
<tr><td>*Dependence on truly tacit knowledge*</td><td>high</td><td>|------|------|------|------|</td><td>low</td></tr>
<tr><td>*Knowledge is teachable*</td><td>not at all</td><td>|------|------|------|------|</td><td>very</td></tr>
<tr><td>*Process has been transferred before*</td><td>never</td><td>|------|------|------|------|</td><td>often</td></tr>
<tr><td>**Customised and obsolete processes**</td><td></td><td></td><td></td></tr>
<tr><td>*Technology is customised, redundant or obsolete*</td><td>very</td><td>|------|------|------|------|</td><td>not at all</td></tr>
<tr><td>*Documentation is up-to-date and representative*</td><td>not at all</td><td>|------|------|------|------|</td><td>very</td></tr>
<tr><td>**Process adaptability**</td><td></td><td></td><td></td></tr>
<tr><td>*Availability of alternatives*</td><td>none</td><td>|------|------|------|------|</td><td>many</td></tr>
<tr><td>*Need for pilot*</td><td>high</td><td>|------|------|------|------|</td><td>low</td></tr>
<tr><td>**Packaging for transfer**</td><td></td><td></td><td></td></tr>
<tr><td>*Ability to transfer SKD or CKD*</td><td>low</td><td>|------|------|------|------|</td><td>high</td></tr>
<tr><td>*Ability to split process into sub-processes*</td><td>low</td><td>|------|------|------|------|</td><td>high</td></tr>
<tr><td>*Ability to protect IPR*</td><td>low</td><td>|------|------|------|------|</td><td>high</td></tr>
</table>

## Worksheet 6. Measuring appropriateness

| **Key factors**<br>*Properties* | Dimensions<br>**Totally inappropriate** – – – – – – – – **Totally appropriate** |
|---:|---|
| **Host labour** | |
| *Productivity and cost of direct/indirect labour* | |
| *Skills available from local labour pool* | |
| *Education and language characteristics* | |
| *Labour turnover* | |
| **Target market** | |
| *Process capacity and flexibility match with target market demand characteristics* | |
| *Product match with target market needs* | |
| **Suppliers** | |
| *Quality, cost, delivery, flexibility and service of local or international suppliers* | |
| **Host infrastructure** | |
| *Quality, cost and availability of local utilities* | |
| *Availability, cost and reliability of telecommunications and transport infrastructure* | |
| *Space and format of buildings* | |
| **Host organisation's resources and capabilities** | |
| *Technical resources* | |
| *Familiarity with manufacturing methods* | |
| *Support capabilities* | |
| *Organisational structure* | |
| **Host culture** | |
| *Degree of individualism and uncertainty avoidance* | |
| *Power distance orientation* | |
| *Working practices* | |
| *Approach to problem solving and quality perception* | |
| **Host environment** | |
| *Local temperature range, humidity and air quality* | |
| **Financing** | |
| *Cost of inventory, cost of land and capital and foreign exchange requirement* | |
| **Host government and legal requirements** | |
| *Legal demands, import duties and quotas, labour laws, approval and licence requirements* | |
| *Government emission regulations and planning laws* | |

## Worksheet 7. Transferring

| Item / knowledge | Transfer mechanism | Purchases required | Approximate cost | Lead-time to host site | Notes |
|---|---|---|---|---|---|
| | | | | | |
| | | | | | |
| | | | | | |
| | | | | | |
| | | | | | |
| | | | | | |
| | | | | | |
| | | | | | |

**Worksheet 8. Potential problem areas for embedding at host site**

| Problem area | Potential for disruption (high/medium/low) | Possible mechanisms for resolution |
|---|---|---|
| | | |
| | | |
| | | |
| | | |
| | | |
| | | |
| | | |
| | | |
| | | |